How To Manage Your Money

An Engrossing Reminder Of The Ways In Which A Relationship Can Be Settled, Improved, Managed, And Balanced Between Couples Who Have Held One's Fortune To Each Other

(A Guide To Making Money For Young People)

Joachim Kemper

TABLE OF CONTENT

Search For Ways To Cut Costs. 1

Formulating A Plan For Building Wealth 4

Productivity And A Positive Attitude..................21

Give Up Changing Your Phone Model 35

What Is A Cash Flow Budget And Cash Flow Management? 50

Address The Issue 65

They Don't Make Regular Investments..............87

What Are Some Fundamentals We Should Understand Before Investing In Options Trading? 105

Search For Ways To Cut Costs.

If you cannot save as much money as you want, it might be time to reduce your spending. Decide which non-essentials you can live without, like entertainment and eating out. Seek ways to reduce the cost of your fixed monthly expenses, including your auto insurance and cell phone plan. Seek out activities that are free of charge as additional recommendations for cutting daily expenses.

Use websites such as local event calendars to find free or inexpensive entertainment.

Analyze reoccurring costs

It is best to cancel memberships and subscriptions set to renew, especially if you are not using them.

Examine the expenses of eating out versus cooking at home.

Make most of your meals at home, and when you do feel like treating yourself, check out the deals at nearby restaurants.

Wait to make a purchase.

When tempted to make an unneeded purchase, wait a few days. It may turn out that you wanted the item instead of needing it, so you may plan to save money for it.

Make a savings plan.

One of the best ways to save money is to set a goal. First, consider your possible long-term (four years or more) and short-term (one to three years) financial goals. Estimate after determining how much money you'll need and how long it might take you to save.

Typical short-term goals include:

A trip.

An emergency fund (three to nine months' worth of expenses).

A down payment on a car.

Common long-term goals, retirement assets, a down payment on a home or renovation project, or your child's education

A quick hint

Set a reasonable, achievable short-term objective for a pleasurable purchase that goes above your monthly budget, such as a new phone or Christmas present. Reaching small goals and indulging in the treat you have been saving for can give you a psychological lift. This reinforces the habit and highlights the advantages of saving.

Configure auto-saving.

Almost everything offers automated transfers between your savings and checking accounts. You have complete control over the location, quantity, and time of money transfers. You can even divide your direct deposit to ensure that a portion of each salary ends up in your savings account.

Watch how your savings grow.

Review your budget and evaluate your progress each month. That will help you stay on track with your personal savings goal and help you quickly recognize and resolve problems.

After learning how to save, you could even be inspired to find other ways to save and reach your goals faster.

In conclusion, saving money is the best and easiest way to increase your income! Saving money ensures a financially secure future and a happy, independent, and peaceful life! As a result, we ought to all set aside some cash.

Formulating A Plan For Building Wealth

Creating a sound wealth-building strategy is one of the most important steps in becoming financially successful. Before starting the procedure, assessing your existing financial status, including your income, expenses, obligations, and assets, is crucial. This assist you in gaining a comprehensive picture of your financial situation and pinpoint areas needing development.

Whichever strategy you choose, it's critical to concentrate on honing abilities and accumulating assets that will eventually produce a steady stream of revenue. Creating a wealth development plan requires careful evaluation of your long-term objectives and present financial status. The steps to developing a wealth-building strategy are as follows:

It's crucial to first establish your financial objectives. Give your long- and short-term goals some thought, and be clear about what you hope to accomplish. This can involve accumulating money for a down payment on a house, paying off debt, or creating a retirement fund, among other things. It's crucial to incorporate a schedule for accomplishing every objective.

Next, assess the state of your finances right now. Examine your earnings, spending, debts, and possessions. Determine your credit score, cash flow, and net worth. This can assist you decide on the best course of action by providing a comprehensive picture of your financial situation.

Make a budget that accounts for your earnings, outlays, and desired level of savings. Prioritize your expenditures according to your financial objectives and be practical.

Building wealth requires first reducing debt. Make a strategy to pay off any high-interest debts as soon as possible after identifying them. If you can, consider combining your loans with a reduced interest rate. By doing this, you'll be able to pay off your bills faster and save money on interest.

The development of an emergency fund is also crucial. Put three to six months' worth of living costs away.

Purchasing a variety of assets is yet another essential stage in accumulating wealth. To diversify your investments and optimize profits. Consult a financial counselor or conduct independent research to find the ideal investment plan for your objectives.

Finally, periodically examine and modify your plan. Make any required adjustments to your plan. This will assist you in staying on course and implementing any required adjustments to meet your financial objectives. You can work toward long-term financial success and wealth accumulation with a sound plan.

Developing money takes time and patience, as well as discipline. Remain committed to your plan, keep your eyes on your objectives, and be ready to modify it as needed. You may attain financial independence and lead the life you want if you have a strong plan for accumulating wealth.

The value of having a strategy in place to increase wealth

Goal clarity: A wealth-building plan assists you in defining your financial objectives and provides a clear path to success. It provides a feeling of purpose and direction, enabling you to decide how best to spend your resources— including income, savings, and investments— toward your objectives.

Financial discipline: A wealth-building strategy offers a structure for responsible money management. It assists with budget creation, spending tracking, systematic saving, and investing, all critical behaviors for long-term wealth accumulation. It helps you stay committed to your long-term objectives and refrain from making snap judgments regarding investing or spending.

Optimizing resources: You may maximize your financial resources by creating a well-thought-out wealth-building plan. By carefully directing your income, savings, and investments toward wealth-building objectives, you ensure you get the most out of them. Based on your financial objectives, it assists you in setting spending, savings, and investment priorities and guarantees that your resources are directed toward accomplishing those objectives.

Risk management: Techniques for controlling risks and safeguarding capital are also included in a wealth-building plan. It could entail building an emergency fund, buying insurance, and diversifying your investments in circumstances like job loss, medical emergencies, or market downturns.

Long-term outlook: Creating money is a long-term project that calls for tolerance and tenacity. A wealth-building plan enables you to see things from a long-term perspective and avoid making rash financial decisions that could endanger your wealth-building objectives. It supports you in maintaining perspective and making wise choices consistent with your long-term financial goals.

Adaptability and flexibility: A strategy for accumulating wealth is not predetermined. It must be evaluated and modified regularly as your financial circumstances and objectives change. It enables you to be adaptive and flexible in response to shifts in the financial markets, the state of the economy, and your circumstances so your wealth-building plan will continue to be relevant and successful.

A well-thought-out plan for accumulating wealth is essential to financial success. It gives you a path forward, supports your discipline, makes the most of your resources, controls risks, cultivates a long-term outlook, and permits flexibility and adaptability. You may take charge of your financial destiny and work toward accumulating wealth for your loved ones and yourself by creating a wealth-building plan.

5. Like Money, Your Financial Intelligence Compounds

You need to increase your financial understanding at least as quickly as your assets. Why?

Furthermore, investing decisions made using a thousand dollars worth of financial knowledge do not carry a higher financial risk than those made with a million dollars.

The ceiling of your financial intelligence constrains your wealth growth. Your financial potential increases as your level of financial literacy rises.

Your investing performance is based on your financial experience or lack thereof.

By learning to invest more frequently, you should enhance your investment and minimize losses when inevitable mistakes are made. That translates to more money and greater steadiness in your pocketbook.

It is a little-known fact about financial intelligence that expands and changes like capital. There are several effects, not just one.

Each new fact adds to the body of knowledge by connecting with everything else. Not only does it add up, but it also grows through geometric multiplication.

The goal is to make weekly deposits into the financial intelligence account in the same manner as you make monthly deposits into your investment accounts.

Your financial knowledge should grow and mature before your investment accounts do.

Taking Charge by Learning About Finances

M

Make advantage of these techniques right now to receive financial support. You might require assistance in line with your objectives if you are caught in a debt cycle, make too little money to live up to your ideal standard, or wish to start saving for a big purchase like a house or an investment. Put these strategies into practice immediately to gain financial control.

Look for the financial advice of specialist books if you need financial aid but don't know where to begin.

Many books are available on money management, debt relief, and portfolio development. Books offer the ideal means of enhancing the financial planning approach.

Get secondhand financial books online or check them out for free from your neighborhood library to increase your savings. If you'd rather listen to advice, think about audiobooks.

Establish a Budget

Your monthly spending plan should be based on your average income and expenses, so if you're having trouble managing your money, you should create a budget. The only way to attain better financial futures is with a budget.

To get your discretionary spending, enter your income and costs first, then deduct your expenses from your revenue. Make a budget each month to determine how to use your discretionary income. At the end of the month, evaluate whether you adhered to the plan by keeping track of your spending.

Reducing unnecessary expenses or making money if you spend more than you brought in will help you balance the budget. Put the revised budget into action for the following month to stay within your limits.

While you can't cut permanent expenditures like rent or auto insurance without drastically altering your lifestyle, you can cut variable costs like entertainment and clothes by being resourceful and flexible.

For instance, you can choose between various home or life insurance companies, minimize your power usage to lower your energy expenses, or purchase food at a discount from bulk retailers.

Give Up Eating Out

Are you trying to find an easy way to monitor your variable charges each month? Reduce the amount you eat. Treating yourself to a fancy meal occasionally is wonderful, but you can save money if you keep cooking at home or bring your lunch to work instead of eating out every day.

At least once a week, start preparing simple meals at home. The following week, keep taking your lunch to work. It could surprise you how much money you can save. By doing this, you will save $1.500 a year, or over $50,000 throughout a 40-year career.

Eliminate Debt

Pay off your debt as quickly as you can so that you can make financial adjustments and acquire additional capital.

Start by listing all the debt you already owe, including credit cards, student loans, and auto loans. Then, figure out the least amount you must pay each month to stay current. Naturally, paying off your debt fully won't help you get out of it quickly. Instead, consider your fixed costs and decide how much of your income you can devote to debt repayment.

Try to negotiate a lower interest rate with the lender, combine several loans into one, or like a balance transfer card, to reduce the debt's interest rate. Then, to pay off the debt as quickly as possible, create a plan to start making wise spending decisions.

Take Care of Your Student Loans

If you do not make proactive payments on your student loans, they may cause you to incur debt over time. It is a great idea to get student debts under control as soon as possible to increase finance, regardless of whether you need to refinance them, combine them, or add them to a debt payment schedule if you qualify for a student loan payback program.

Your loan repayment schedule doesn't need to be drastically altered; you will make a complete extra payment per year and pay half of your student loan every two weeks. Enrolling in automated loan payments can potentially result in a 0.25% interest rate reduction from some lenders.

Establish a Budget

You need to have a financial plan to manage your money and reach your goals. A financial plan is, in essence, a road map for the major turning points in your life.

This is similar to a budget, but instead of being a short-term plan for the upcoming weeks or months, this covers a longer time frame of 10, twenty, or three decades. Every document functions as a whole, and the budget plays a significant role in a larger financial plan.

Since focusing on one or two financial goals at a time is always more productive, these tactics can also assist you in managing your funds. Your financial plan will cover house ownership, retirement savings, and your kids' schooling.

Establish sensible objectives

Set financial goals, like buying a house or increasing your retirement savings, and give it some thought. You won't be able to inspire yourself to save or invest money each month if you don't have any specific tasks.

Make sure your goals are reachable before you establish them. First, if your annual salary is merely $30,000, don't aim to pay off $40,000 in debt in a single year. Your unrealistic expectations for failure will keep you from making the correct financial decisions.

Lastly, create a goal chart to track your progress toward your goals over time. For instance, the websites of most contemporary brokerage firms provide facilities for tracking the gains and losses in your investment portfolio. With the help of these instruments, you may monitor a long-term objective.

Safeguard Your Funds

Take steps to safeguard your savings from yourself if you're good at saving money each month but find it easy to dip into them to make up for a gap in your expenditure or seize an opportunity.

Creating an emergency fund at a different bank than you usually do is one way to find a solution, as is transferring your money from a physical bank with easily accessible funds to an online bank with less liquidity.

Game 1: Charades: Making Decisions

Playing this game is a great method to get comfortable telling people what you've decided.

1. Make two teams out of the players.

2. Every team selects a decision that one player will act out.

3. The team's other players attempt to predict the outcome.

4. The first team to make the most decisions wins the game!

Example from real life: Some teenage lads are playing Charades de Décision. One boy acts out the choice of whether to ask a girl out on a date. The other boys attempt to predict the outcome. Without uttering a word, the boy enacting the decision tries to provide hints. Based on the hints, the boys on the opposing team attempt to determine the outcome. Until one team guesses the most decisions, the game goes on.

Game 2: The Dominoes That Make Decisions

Playing this game is a great method to learn about the various aspects of making decisions.

1. Assemble a set of dominoes and write various elements on them, like "Your values," "Your goals," "Your emotions," and "The opinions of others."

2. The dominoes should be shuffled and laid face down.

3. One by one, turn over two dominoes.

4. If the two dominoes match, you must decide according to the criteria indicated on the dominoes.

5. You must draw another domino if the two do not match.

6. Until one player has made a particular amount of decisions, the game goes on.

An example story to help you relate: Dominoes is a game played by an adolescent male. He topples two dominoes over. The boy must choose a course of action that aligns with his values and goals when the first domino reads "Your values" and the second says "Your goals." He decides to prepare for his test since he understands how essential a quality education is to him.

With these exercises and games, I hope you can put the goal-setting skills in this book into practice. They are an entertaining and interesting approach to practicing making wise decisions and learning about decision-making.

Productivity And A Positive Attitude

About one-third of your life is spent at work. Spending it with negative individuals has the potential to seriously affect and depress you.

You'll do a lot of the work to stay optimistic in a bad situation and develop your business skills by recording negative thoughts as soon as they occur and resisting the need to act on them.

Techniques to prevent startling events at work from getting in the way of you.

Maintain a daily life apart from your job.

Retain coworkers who are somewhat grounded in reality and with whom you may discuss matters of life that are completely unrelated to your job.

Refuse to discuss work-related topics outside of work hours, particularly if the atmosphere is toxic and not only about your ideas.

Recognize that most of what goes on is work-related and that most negativity directed at you isn't directed at you.

Consider the strain your colleagues are under as they grind away in their own lives at home, and recognize that they are anticipating the worst and projecting their resentment onto you and those around them. Remember that being a businessperson requires having the ability to manage people.

Refuse to allow your partners' self-centered lead, aspirations, and compulsive worker to permeate your system.

It is simple to start letting bad information seep in by endorsing one side or agreeing with opposing viewpoints. Perhaps choose to transcend all of it by staying impartial.

Watch what you think about it because, ultimately, it will become real to you. Make sure your mind doesn't continue to replay the negativity that surrounds you. If you believe it helps you focus, turn on some music at a reasonable volume in your workspace. Take pauses to collect your thoughts. Maintain perfect updates regarding what you are trying to study and accomplish in the statements and images surrounding your workspace.

Thoroughly consider your options for launching your entrepreneurial journey. Some managers may be detrimental; if the organizational environment doesn't appear to be changing, determine if this is the best place for you and consider how you can launch your business soon.

You spend eight or more hours a day at your desk answering calls, sending messages, and reading correspondence. Things go like this: the stack of papers on your disorganized desk keeps getting larger, you eat more dinners at work than at home, and you still barely meet your deadlines.

Look for ways to stay out of time traps, improve your already-existing tactics to be more productive but much less focused at work, and develop skills you may use in your own company.

Observation time killers: Common offenders include texting, internet browsing, making individual calls, and gossiping with companions. The minutes devoted to these misreadings could turn into extended periods of lost time and productivity loss.

Establish boundaries for these pursuits and devise polite ways to conclude conversations.

Minimize interference and disruptions.

Set aside time to respond to voice, email, and letter correspondence and to follow up. Turn off moment courier apps whenever you can, and avoid taking individual calls while working on other jobs.

Arrange and concentrate on.

If you frequently search your disorganized workspace, give yourself enough time to organize documents, tools, and hardware. Both paper and digital records should be kept in sealed envelopes. Create shortcuts and other options on your computer to help you find things easily and fast.

Keep track of all events, deadlines, and meetups with a single, compact schedule.

Make a schedule for when to start and finish a task and follow it.

Start and finish tasks on time. Additionally, a daily or weekly timetable can be a helpful tool for maintaining attention and productivity.

Chapter 6: Safeguarding Your Money

Effective money management requires you to safeguard your assets. This is taking precautions to reduce financial risk and protect assets from unforeseen circumstances. We'll talk about money protection tactics in this chapter.

Fund for Emergencies

Making an emergency fund is one of the most crucial financial safety measures. This savings account is intended to cover unforeseen costs like auto or medical repairs. Ideally, you should have three to six months' worth of living expenditures in your emergency fund.

Protection

Another essential instrument for safeguarding your finances is insurance. Your home, car, and health insurance can help you budget for unforeseen expenses. To guard against potential hazards, consider getting life, long-term care, or disability insurance.

Planning an Estate

Estate planning is preparing for how your possessions will be divided when you die. This can involve naming beneficiaries for your life insurance and retirement savings, setting trusts and wills, and minimizing tax consequences for your heirs.

Protection Against Identity Theft

In the digital age, identity theft is becoming a more serious issue. Your credit report, and stay off public Wi-Fi networks when accessing sensitive data to safeguard your finances against identity theft.

Fraud Defense

Your finances could potentially be at risk from fraud. You can guard against fraud by looking for shady emails, phone calls, and bank statements and immediately report any unusual behavior to your financial institutions.

Investment Protection: There is a chance that investments could put you at risk financially. Consider engaging with a financial advisor to safeguard your investments. They can assist you in making wise selections and in routinely reviewing your portfolio. Do your research before investing in any offer, and stay alert for financial fraud.

In summary

Maintaining financial security is a continuous effort that calls for care and attention to detail. You may reduce your financial risks and preserve your assets by setting up an emergency fund, getting insurance, arranging your estate, guarding against fraud and identity theft, and keeping an eye on your investments. To make wise financial decisions, keep yourself informed and, when needed, seek professional advice.

AMAZING SOLUTIONS TO END YOUR DEBT!

Some people may struggle to make ends meet when paying their debts and other financial commitments. This can leave them helpless and increase their financial difficulties and complexity, affecting other areas of their lives, like losing their homes or being sued.

The main cause is the adoption of absurd financial practices and conventions. Thus, having a solid financial plan enables you to meet your financial commitments and pay off your debts as soon as possible, allowing you to live a debt-free life. These six actions could assist you in permanently resolving your debt problem.

Six methods to assist with debt repayment:

1. A powerful will, step forward, champion!

One of the most crucial elements in properly planning your finances and carrying out your plans despite obstacles is willingness. Deciding to break certain bad financial habits is the most challenging aspect.

Therefore, set a challenge for yourself and prioritize paying off your debt above everything else. This will allow you to pay off your debt immediately, use your income for other essentials, and save some for the future.

2. Refrain from incurring extra costs. Become the more astute one!

No matter how little money you spend, you should always make sure that it is helping you. To do this, go over your spending and identify the methods in which you spend it, eliminating unnecessary items from your budget or substituting them with less expensive options.

For instance, if you want financing from a bank or financing company, you must compare the costs of the financing products offered by those agencies. The most crucial comparisons are the cost-term and the annual percentage rate (APR), which are required by the monetary institution to be disclosed to give customers the information they need to determine which financing products are less expensive.

3. Raise the monthly payment amount designated for debt repayment.

Increasing the amount you set aside each month to pay off your debts will help you pay them off faster, especially if they are expensive loans. The loan repayment period will shorten when the monthly savings amount increases, meaning no further interest will be needed.

High-cost debts should, therefore, be paid off first because failing to do so will incur additional penalties and costs.

4. Refuse to accept the bare minimum of credit cards

Regarding credit cards, some people might be lax and simply pay the minimal amount due in full, resulting in interest accruing due to deferring the payment and paying interest on top of the remaining balance due the following month. To avoid monthly interest charges, you must pay the entire balance owed on your credit cards when the due date arrives.

5. Ask for assistance, have an open mind, and work with a financial advisor!

Analyze your financial position and guide appropriate behavior in such circumstances if your low salary, job loss, approaching retirement age, or an emergency financial crisis prevents you from paying your debts and financial obligations, causing your financial situation to change. In this context, it is important to note that, per the Monetary Agency's 2014 guidelines for protecting bank customers, most banks worldwide must offer credit counseling services to their clients without charging extra or receiving financial compensation. This is meant to assist defaulters and support them in navigating the financial crisis with as little negative impact as possible.

6. Look for appropriate banking services and solutions; a brilliant researcher has a bright future.

Look for services and solutions suitable for your needs and financial situation if you accumulate debts due to using multiple credit cards excessively or getting multiple financing products at once and are unable to pay new financial obligations.

Typically, banks offer a variety of goods and solutions to meet the demands of all clientele groups. Also, avoid making poor decisions that will worsen your financial crisis, such as turning to unlicensed financial agencies to settle your debts. Some crisis traders prey on people in financial distress, accusing them of larger debts or trapping them in unrelated scams.

Give Up Changing Your Phone Model

It amazes me how frequently individuals tell me they need a new phone. I have even overheard folks say that to someone over the phone! Well, to whom are you talking if your phone isn't working?

I am aware that, against popular belief, you shouldn't replace your phone every few years in this day and age.

Your current phone should last you at least 4 or 5 years before it decides to give up on you if you just take excellent care of it. And since phones cost up to $1,000, this small piece of advice could save you a lot of money.

II

The Benefits of Setting a Budget

However, suppose you've never lived on a budget or taken advantage of all the advantages budgeting provides. In that case, you might wonder why this is such a crucial part of your finances. What makes budgeting so crucial, then?

In the remaining sections of this book, I'll go into much more detail on the value of budgeting and why it's crucial to your financial health. Now, let's get going!

8 Budgeting Assists in Managing Your Expenditure

To be honest, nothing can prevent you from overspending when managing your funds without a budget. Of course, you might have a rough notion of how much you must spend each month, but without precise and reliable data, it's challenging to rein in your spending patterns. I'd be aware of it. I wasted money like it was nothing before deciding to start budgeting. It was hard to balance living costs with the dire financial circumstances without a budget, whether eating out or hiking in the mountains. Of course, purchasing a single burrito at a time isn't a huge concern. However, when you get down with a budget and figure out how much 30 Chipolata Burritos cost a month—yes, thirty—those seemingly little expenses quickly mount up to an excessive amount. Put another way, budgeting is essential if you wish to monitor your daily spending patterns, comprehend the significance of even seemingly insignificant purchases, and exercise financial restraint.

A LIST TO HELP YOU SET YOUR INTEREST RATE] If you are unsure whether you have any loans with variable interest rates, check studentaid.gov or your Chapter 1 Personal Student Loan chart.

Check the current interest rate on any variable rate loans you have by visiting the Department of Education's website at https://studentaid.gov/help-center/answers/article/what-is-current-interest-rate-for-direct-unsubsidized-loans. When you consolidate your student loans; this rate will apply to the component with a variable interest rate.

⌐ To find the weighted average of your student loans, multiply each loan's percentage of your total loans by the associated interest rate. After that, total all the outcomes to see your interest rate on a combined loan.

Consolidate your variable rate loans so you may set aside money each month, knowing the payment will remain the same until the loan is repaid in full.

Further Advantages of Consolidation

While one of the main advantages of loan consolidation is being able, this is not the only one.

One Single Payment

Having just one monthly payment to make has always been the main advantage of consolidation. Why is this advantageous if your debt remains the same? How well you keep your accounts plays a part in determining your credit score. You are, therefore, less likely to forget to make a payment and lower your credit score if you have just one.

Additionally, one loan may go between the cracks, and you may forget about it if you have eight separate loans. I'm positive that I did. Except for one loan that I completely forgot about and defaulted, all of my other loans were in forbearance. My debt was in default, so I had to wait for it to be approved for consolidation until I made enough payments. However, I never missed another loan payment after consolidating my debt and paying a few late payments. Five years have passed. I have a single loan payment deducted directly from my account every month.

Reasonably Priced Extended Payments

Lower payments are beneficial if your student loan debt is at least $40,000. Even while you might not need all 25 years to pay off your loan, there are situations in which you might find that the smaller payment is helpful:

• Should you wish to purchase a home. To determine if you are a good lending risk, banks use your credit scores and the total monthly loan payments. • In the event of a significant change in your life, reduced payments also increase your likelihood of being able to afford your mortgage. A few significant life events that can affect your finances are losing your job, getting married, having a baby, or experiencing a health issue.

PART THREE: DIFFERENT KINDS OF INVESTMENTS

Investing your money is a wise way to use it for your benefit and perhaps increase in value over time. The absolute most common types of investments are as follows:

1. Stocks: Buying an organization's stock essentially means buying a portion of that business. The value of your parts may rise as

the company expands and becomes more successful. However, the value of stocks can decrease, and they can also be unpredictable.

2. Bonds: Bonds are credits you grant to states or organizations bond's assumed value. Although they typically offer lower expected returns than stocks, bonds are generally considered safer than equities.

3. Real Estate: Purchasing real estate, such as houses, commercial buildings, or land, is one way to invest in real estate. After a while, real estate may gain value in addition to rental income. Either way, it usually comes with rising support fees and demands a large upfront investment.

4. Mutual Assets: Shared reserves combine funds from multiple investors to invest in a broader range of stocks, bonds, and other assets. They are a well-known option for certain financial backers because they are

enhanced and managed by skilled asset supervisors.

5. Exchange-Traded Funds (ETFs): TRADED on stock exchanges like individual equities, ETFs are similar to common assets. Because they are less expensive, they can be more useful and provide a wider perspective.

6. Certificates of Deposit (CDs): CDs are interest-bearing savings accounts offered by banks with set durations that might range from a few months to an extended period. They provide a projected return, although generally speaking, their interest rates are lower than those of other investments.

7. Savings Accounts: One of the most basic investing options banks offer is a savings account. It provides a safe place to save money and often has a low interest rate. For short-term savings goals and crisis assets, this is a great choice.

Commodities include real goods like gold, oil, and agricultural supplies. Investors can exchange product prospects or directly invest in real resources. Products can grow, but natural market forces can also impact them.

9. Subsidiaries and Options: Subordinates and options are financial contracts that derive value from a basic resource, such as bonds or equities. They are more complex and can be applied theoretically or as a safeguard against anticipated bad luck.

10. Cryptocurrencies: As optional investments, sophisticated money forms such as Ethereum and Bitcoin have gained prominence. They face extreme cost uncertainty and are highly speculative.

11. Retirement Accounts: Long-term retirement savings can benefit from tax advantages from retirement accounts such as 401(k)s and IRAs. Shared reserves may be included.

Peer-to-peer lending systems allow individuals to lend money to borrowers in return for interest payments. This brings us to number twelve. Although it's an optional pay creation method, a credit risk is involved.

Why is knowledge about discretionary money important or necessary? If you are unsure of your spending limit, you are more likely to go over it. Your only option for budgeting maybe with this understanding. How much of your money is discretionary?

1. Note every source of income, including side gigs and principal (primary) employment. To determine your overall revenue, add them all together. 2. Make a list of every category you spend money on Housing (Rent or Mortgage)

Services

Food

Individualised Care

Medical Care

Amusement

Conserve

Debt

3. You can enter each category's average expenses or total. When categorizing each thing, you should be quite precise. Attending the cinema is for amusement, not for self-care.

4. Total your expenses by adding the amounts from each section.

5. You may calculate your discretionary income using this easy maths: Your total income plus all your expenses equals your discretionary income.

Was the result of this number good or negative? Whether or not it was bad is irrelevant. This is where your journey begins. If your negative programming tells you that this investigation is too difficult and that you should avoid it, there is still hope. Determine your monthly income and deduct it from the amount due each month from your bank account balance. You can estimate your spending with this strategy, even though it is not a reliable accounting technique.

Why is having more money essential to you? Others will make a strategy if you have positive income (positive discretionary income) and none. By doing this exercise, you might be able to determine the reason(s) behind your negative discretionary income. If you're daring, split your total spending and income. This will display the amount of money you have spent in a particular month.

It's acceptable to choose not to make any budgets. Your monthly discretionary income will be known to you. Avoid doing so, as it may result in costly and needless debt. It might also lead to overspending. You may have to use your credit card, which will cut into your disposable income and raise your debt payments.

This activity could be time-consuming, difficult, or wasteful if negative thinking is present. Try to think of it as a multipurpose tool rather than something that takes time, is too hard, or is a waste of time. You might cease depending entirely on your credit card to cover the voids. You may discover places for improvement.

Consider discretionary income as a source of revenue rather than as tedious budget geek maths. It is the starting point for making a customized spending plan. You can utilize it to better understand your lifestyle as well. At this step, you can select one of the three models that most closely matches your requirements and tastes.

ACTION ITEM

Do you still object to the exercise of discretionary income? Maybe you don't believe knowing is necessary. Maybe you detested the idea or the practice more than the conclusion. Consider visualizing something. This can assist you in changing your viewpoint. What was the main motivation for the first action item's budget creation? Which was the main explanation you gave?

That concludes it. List the five things you would most like to have. Would you like to establish an education fund or a retirement fund? How can you put money aside for house renovations or a car? Methods for Paying Off Debt: Increasing your money for fun and discretion? Maybe you only want a little additional cash to spend on fun things. Who wouldn't want to embark on a far-off adventure?

After completing that, picture yourself achieving your objectives. Then, consider whether any of these are worthwhile investments. Next, evaluate which is most difficult and which is easiest. Next, order your objectives by significance. Do you still want to accomplish the original goal of the first action item?

A deadline can never be set. To begin, determine if the objectives on your list, including your primary goal, are short-term or long-term. If necessary, you can make a different list using these titles:

Short-term objectives (1 to 6 months)

Mid-term objectives (six to twelve months)

Long-term objectives (one to five years).

How do you plan to accomplish your objectives? Any task requires a plan to be completed. Dividing any task into manageable chunks is a lot simpler. The main goal of this workbook is self-empowerment. This can be accomplished by deciding your objectives and then acting to meet them. You can use these objectives as a guide to help you develop and oversee a spending plan and budget. It will be beneficial. Your actions will reflect your ability to see yourself achieving those objectives. You will be rewarded for your sacrifices, and they will be appreciated.

A timetable can be made when you've given your goals some thought and determined which one you want to accomplish. Next, ascertain the financial requirements to make it materialize. Next, maintain your primary objective in focus. Next, decide which spending strategy will assist you in reaching your objective.

What Is A Cash Flow Budget And Cash Flow Management?

If money is involved, timing is everything. People often find that they have an extra week, so they pay many bills at once or indulge in pleasant activities, only to run out of money the next day when they need to buy something vital.

Integrates the time of your income and expenses in dollar numbers for each line item, setting it apart from an average budget. Using a cash flow budget, you can identify your monthly deficiencies.

Using it, you can ensure you have enough cash to cover essential expenses like rent and stay out of debt. You can use a cash flow budget to target areas efficiently. It might help you plan and project how to allocate your funds throughout the months you will have none. Cash flow budgeting. The process of establishing a cash flow budget involves three steps:

1. Keep track of your earnings and outgoing costs for one, two, or three weeks.

2. Examine your spending.

3. Using this information to create a cash flow budget. A calendar for cash flow. The primary purpose of your cash flow budget is to set goals for how you will use your revenue going forward.

Do Your Taxes to Prevent a Bill.

I am not talking about filing your taxes on time.

You should know exactly what taxes you must pay to ensure you pay the right amount and are not hit with a bill.

It makes no difference how much income you make from other sources, whether you have a second job or are on maternity or parental leave, when figuring out how much income you should be paying in taxes.

Verify that your employer, the government, or the financial institution is responsible for your taxes.

Remember that if your maternity leave extends beyond two calendar years, you must do this calculation again. Regardless of where your income comes from, you must ensure you set aside enough for taxes and not face a payment that will strain your budget.

Don't Tithe if You Have Debts

Do you still give to charities or tithe when you're in debt? Give no more; that is not your money.

I don't mind providing money as long as it makes you happy. Because it's your money, make a choice. However, you have to pay for it.

That's where I draw the line regarding tithing and charitable contributions. You should only be contributing the tenth if it's your money.

I, therefore, find it difficult to pay tithes when I am in debt.

It's time to start setting aside your needs and pleasures to donate if you feel that tithing is a necessary part of your identity and worldview.

Refuse the new jumper, the vacation, and the coffee. Invest financial resources with genuine giving. So be it if a sacrifice is required. It requires you to lay out your financial plan.

It is impossible to tithe your own money if you are in debt. Lenders worldwide, who stand to gain handsomely from your contribution, endorse your "gift." Being responsible means making sure you live within your means.

It is not your place to tithe to appease your conscience. Tithing is only permitted for those who are financially secure.

It is hypocritical to tithe exactly the amount prescribed and then utilize a monthly amount from your credit line because you are not donating.

Next, you have to use your resources to tithe. Sharing does not always imply money. You may discuss your experience.

Anything you own is exchangeable, including anything you bought with credit. For someone else to have what you would be prepared to give up?

Saving Money While Eliminating Debt

It is imperative to settle the debt. Developing a saving habit is also important. Getting to the point of financial stability just takes one step.

If you don't handle your money in a balanced manner, you will run out of money. Use the extra money to pay off debt until you have none left. It's important to put paying off debt before preserving financial stability. You want to be debt-free permanently, of course. Planning is necessary.

Additionally, equilibrium is required. Making decisions and committing to things that will negatively impact other areas of your financial life is unwise. If you don't start saving for emergencies, you'll use credit when things go bad. Put off creating a very helpful habit without investing. Is there ever a suitable time to begin making financial savings?

This is the perfect time to begin saving! And okay, so be it if accomplishing that means setting aside $1 per day.

To pay off your debt as soon as possible, keep the other elements of your financial plan intact, including your goals, spending plan, emergency fund, insurance, and estate plan.

If you want to pay off your debt rapidly, take on a second job, a third one, and so on. Crack your ass. Hold onto your savings.

Chapter 5: Put money aside for unexpected expenses.

Overview

Saving money shouldn't be limited to covering your future educational expenses. You ought to keep cash on hand in case of emergencies. This can help you avoid borrowing money from your parents or friends. This also allows you to avoid taking out a loan that could result in further debt. Thus, save aside some funds for unexpected expenses, as this could have an impact.

How to Reserve Funds for Unexpected Needs.

Setting aside money for an emergency may not be an easy task to complete. You could, however, think about other approaches. These are listed in the following order:

• Maintain an emergency fund in a different account.

If you have trouble setting aside money for emergencies, you can consider separating your money. A portion of your funds should be set aside for unanticipated expenses and emergencies. This will help you ensure you don't waste money on unnecessary things.

• Transfer funds to your bank account.

Put money into your bank account if you are tempted to spend it on various things. After you have put money into your bank account, avoid checking it frequently, as this may urge you to spend it just on purchases, which could result in extra expenses over your budget. Therefore, transfer the funds straight into your bank account if you don't want to use your emergency savings for unnecessary and non-beneficial items.

Saving money can be accomplished easily by thinking about the items mentioned above. Therefore, if you desire the money, you can use it for emergencies without relying on others; remember the previously mentioned people.

The benefits of emergency fund accumulation.

You will benefit in many ways once you have set aside a percentage of your funds for emergencies. One benefit is that you won't have to take out loans, which could increase your expenses. Thanks to this, you'll be able to refrain from taking out loans from your friends or parents. The best thing about keeping money on hand for emergencies is that you may use it whenever necessary to accomplish important goals. All you need to do if you have this money is take it out of your safe or withdraw it.

While some students may not need to set aside money for emergencies, doing so could assist them avoid incurring more expenses or debt because they will be using their savings rather than their expensive current budget.

Learn How to Use That Smartphone.

These days, every person possesses this amazing device known as a "cell phone," which has a higher registering power than the PC that was used to send people to the moon in the first place. You will become more valuable if you learn how to use the devices, such as list keeping, shut and shutoffs, etc.

Keep Track of Shows

If you enjoy watching TV, invest in a DVR or similar system to record the episodes you want to watch later, when you're free, instead of when they air.

Modify the Organisation

If you put in the effort to organize things to improve your life, it may start to feel robotic if you just make organizing and cleaning habits. This is how a very large number of people learned how to brush their teeth. It developed into a tendency. Throwing away your trash every time you drink a fresh cup of coffee can also become a habit. When you include small habits into your day, everything will seem to be happening.

Upgrade Your Home's Intelligence

In a good way and according to your instructions, you can now have a house that opens the door for you, turns on the light, preheats the grill, etc. If you can afford to invest in this effective innovation, it's a fantastic way to ensure everything gets done. You may employ technological advancements in mechanization to water your indoor plants or grass.

Hire Domestic Assistance

If you cannot computerize some of your tasks at work, you still have the option to do them at home. Invest in a family computer by hiring someone to complete your household chores every week.

Create Systems

A framework is necessary for everything you know has to be done regularly. Everything is done routine, including bookkeeping, cleaning, and paying bills. To get more coordinated through computerization, frameworks that include innovation, designation, and propensity development should be set up. Every time you look at fresh opportunities to computerize something, consider how long it will take you to complete it, how much it will cost to continue doing manual tasks that can occasionally be automated, and how valuable the task is. Remember that robotization saves you 365 hours a year, even if you only gain an hour back from your day. That exceeds fifteen days. You have fifteen days to do a lot.

Day Nine

Now that the prior task has cleared your target SR, ensure you hit this monthly rate by implementing automated transfers for all your savings contributions.

Saving money can be difficult since, as you've already seen, it's frequently neglected until the end of the month, when you discover how much is still available for savings contributions. Typically, people spend their money early in the month and save the remainder. That implies that saving isn't prioritized and that achieving savings goals could still be hampered by other factors, even with a spending plan.

Even if you have other plans, it can be difficult not to spend money as long as it is in your wallet or bank account. Of course, you lose your goals and resolutions if you spend that money rather than saving it or putting it into an account for retirement.

Thus, let's ensure you consistently meet the savings targets you set for yourself each month and reverse the order: save first, then spend the remainder. Your money is securely locked away when you set up automatic savings payments to be deducted from your checking account at the beginning of each month or immediately after you get paid. This eliminates temptations and justifications for starting savings tomorrow rather than today.

Day Nine Action Plan

Put the money you save each month towards your objectives.

Consider your next month's SR target, which you established on day 8, and calculate the components of those savings: How much will be allocated to every savings goal?

You must save $216 if your take-home salary is $1,800 and your SR is 12% for the upcoming month. How much of this will go towards investments, your retirement fund, and your savings account (or accounts, if that's the case)? Open the bank account that receives your paycheck, then create recurring transfers to your different savings accounts. Set them aside for a day or two following your pay date so that the money is deducted from your account at the beginning of your spending cycle. Set them for your regular pay date instead of the day you usually get paid, as you risk overdrawing your bank account if your employer is a day or two late with their payments.

Per your decision on day 8, you will now raise your SR by 1% every two to three months. Be sure to update your automatic payments with the appropriate amount when that time comes.

Address The Issue

"Consumers are always naturally anxious after purchasing a product" is a statement I make often. They always worry, I promise, that they have overspent, made rash decisions, or wasted money. Remember that your task is to completely and promptly remove this buyer's regret. People will probably have questions about your product or service, so always try your best to respond. Create a Q&A page. Help them install the software if that's what it is. Give them the chance to ask questions about specific areas if it's an e-book. Every product or service you offer will inevitably elicit queries from consumers.

Remember that you must be there for them during this initial questioning to gain their trust and have a shot at future sales.

After a transaction, the real job begins. Continue to serve your consumer base. Don't just disappear.

Ensure your help desk software is up and running at all times and that clients receive prompt answers to their inquiries. Consider creating a round-the-clock support system; they are inexpensive and genuinely helpful. When someone submits a request, it's a good idea to automatically send them a message verifying that the request has been received and will be handled as quickly as possible.

If your product is rather complex, you might want to create a YouTube video or provide a video tutorial that you can post on your website to help users understand how to use it. This can appear on your thank-you page following payment processing. Include your company's complete contact information so inquiries can be made. This is when you should try to be as approachable as possible to your audience.

Why take on this whole task? Because your client is new to you and has only recently bought a product. You must demonstrate your unwavering commitment to offering assistance following the transaction. This will improve the customer's chances and give them the impression that you offer them quality service.

CHAPTER 8: There Are Not Many Seconds Left

Indeed, there is a fierce rivalry, and many people are on the Internet. Because you invested time developing your brand and business, website visitors owe you nothing. You have only a few seconds to make that sweet sale, and the best you can hope for is a few seconds of their attention before they leave your website and never bother to visit it again. Never forget that you must show the competition why you are superior to them in those few seconds.

For several examples, the most effective technique to capture the reader's attention is not with flashing arrows or garish graphics—of course, use them sparingly. Glitzy customers are not the kind who will stick with you in the long run; sooner or later, someone else will come along with a flashier website and capture their interest. Providing high-quality content and attending to your clients from the moment they visit your website is the best method to establish a sustainable competitive advantage over your rivals.

I've put up a short list of ideas to get you thinking about your website and how you might separate from the competition and take the initiative:

You must always show that you deserve the top spot on the Internet for your particular subject. You are the greatest at what you do, and there should be no question about that in the market. You cannot ever allow your clients' expectations to be unmet. Spread the word as much as possible online since you may respond to client inquiries and answer questions on blogs and forums. You'll find yourself one step ahead of the competition after this procedure, which may take some time, but that's where you should be.

Make sure your pricing plan is obvious. If you undercut your competitors and provide a lower price than they do, you can eventually drive yourself out of business. Just because an e-book costs $47 doesn't mean it's worth that much. You want clients who downloaded your files or paid for your services to feel they received good value for their money. You must offer more value if your pricing is higher than your rivals. It all comes down to keeping your word.

Remember that your website isn't a static, inert money machine. You must continuously release updated versions of your items and look for better ways to improve them. To develop new ideas for managing your business and promoting your items, try split testing, time-limited promotions, and providing free samples to gauge consumer demand. Like the Internet,

internet marketing is always changing, and your business should, too.

Recall that acquiring new customers is more expensive than maintaining existing ones. Never undervalue the importance of a loyal consumer. Ensure that the people who have bought your goods or services are well cared for. Pay close attention to customer grievances and respond promptly to their questions and concerns. Remember that your clients are strangers to you and are unaware of your wonderful qualities. You must demonstrate this by attending to their needs. Your money-back guarantees must always be honored exactly as you promised: without fuss, without inquiry, and delay. Whether the issue is related to technical challenges or customer service, your objective is to respond to all support tickets in less than a day. If you were the customer, you would have the same expectations.

Keep an eye on what your clients desire. Look at other websites, blogs, and forums to discover what people request. It's not like you try to force people to buy your preferred goods. Instead, concentrate on giving them what they desire. Don't be scared to occasionally look after your unborn child. Declare that you've improved a product by doing something outstanding. Consumers are watching you, and you'll win their respect and business if they notice that you've included one of their ideas in your next offering.

Recognize your rivals. This holds for all types of businesses, including those that offer computers, dry cleaners, and doughnuts. You are never going to be taken off guard. Subscribe to the newsletters of your rivals, observe their marketing tactics, and determine which ones you can use. Observe your surroundings to determine whether you are meeting the needs of your consumers promptly enough or if you need to change course.

Section 2. How is a Credit Score Determined?

Multiple credit report components are used to compute your credit score. Knowing how credit is determined and which institutions (banks and credit agencies) must approve or deny a loan or credit card is essential for excellent credit.

These criteria are used to determine your credit score, specifically:

The sums you are in debt for

The Payment's past

Which categories of open accounts do you have?

The accounts' age

The number of applications for credit

Let's examine these elements and see how we might improve your credit score individually.

The Total Amounts You Owe

The fact that the amount you owe is the subject of conversation after this is no accident. This is because it is recognized as the aspect that influences your credit score the most after your payment history.

As it is, you are only allowed to spend thirty percent of the credit that the bank approves, no more. Using all the credit the bank authorizes— say $300 on a $1000 credit card—would be foolish. This implies that you should never use your card's maximum account amount.

When you begin to rely on the money, credit bureaus take this as a bad indicator and tend to remove you because it reflects poorly on your credit report and credit score.

I recommend utilizing no more than 30% of your credit limit or, even better, using 10% of your credit line and nothing more. Doing this will give you higher credit ratings and endless opportunities to raise and maintain your credit score.

Another important thing to consider when determining your score is how much money you owe.

The Payment History

Since it is crucial and will significantly affect your score, consider paying on time or earlier.

Whether or not you paid your payments or even your credit loans on time is the main thing a lender wants to know. Paying attention to this category is crucial since making it the one that affects it the most out of all the others.

Now that you know how late payments establish a positive credit history, you must pay off your bills without hesitation and on time.

The accounts that are often taken into consideration for payment history are as follows:

Installment Loans

Credit cards (such as Mastercard, Visa, and so on)

Consumer loans

retail accounts, in addition to

Home Loans

Recall that maintaining and raising your credit score will necessitate timely payment.

Which Open Account Types Do You Own?

Having a variety of debts, including credit cards and loans for vehicles, homes, and education, can also help your credit score.

The many forms of credit you use—credit cards, home loans, installment loans, and accounts with finance companies—primarily affect your credit score.

Remember that using them all is unnecessary, and I suggest you just create the accounts you intend to use.

While your credit mix does not impact your credit score much, the surplus information in your credit report—the basis for your score— mustn't be present.

A credit mix is never ideal since it changes over time and depends on the individual. Getting credit cards, auto loans, or education loans you won't need is not a good idea.

Possessing this evidence of your ability to manage your credit responsibly would be a bonus.

The Accounts' Age

Your credit score will always be high if you continue to have a strong credit history. According to the general rule, your credit score rises the longer you have credit cards. I'll tell you to start building credit as soon as you can because of this. This component, roughly 15% of your credit score, assesses how long you've had credit accounts and how effectively you've handled them.

What your FICO credit score indicates is as follows:

It considers the average age of all your new and old accounts.

It also considers the length of time you have been with them, the state of your payment history, and any credit lines you may have.

Lastly, it determines the precise age of your credit cards and debts. Because of this, many experts suggest against canceling or closing older accounts because they will probably lower your credit score.

Obtaining credit for a lengthy period increases your chances of obtaining a high credit score.

Effective Work Practices

- The Benefits of Dedicated Work

One cannot emphasize the importance of single-tasking in a society that frequently exalts multitasking. We are constantly led to believe that multitasking is ideal. In any case, let me assure you that it isn't. Be an expert at one thing rather than an idiot at several. When you single-task, you give the task at hand your whole attention, which promotes deeper engagement and comprehension. This depth fosters a feeling of mastery and achievement, which increases self-assurance and drive. It's a surefire way to choose quality over quantity and accomplish what you do well.

Additionally, focusing on only one job at a time reduces mental clutter. It does this by making your mental processes simpler and your actions more efficient, which lowers stress. Rather than trying to multitask, your mind is focused, clear, and prepared to take on one activity at a time. This clarity enhances decision-making, creativity, and problem-solving skills. Ultimately, single-tasking is powerful because it can help you reach your full potential, produce better work, and cultivate mindfulness in all you do.

Myths about Batch Processing and Multitasking

The Myth of Batch Processing

A common source of myths about batch processing is misinterpreting what it involves. Some could see it as an unbending, rigid process that stifles spontaneity and innovation. This impression is not accurate, though. Batch processing is an organized method that increases concentration and production rather than being mechanical. It enables people to group related jobs together to maximize productivity and reduce distractions. When you group related things, you're setting aside specific time slots to do them, facilitating a flow state that improves performance. The myth fails to recognize that batch processing offers an adaptable framework that allows you to prioritize and adjust activities within each batch, encouraging innovation and adaptability within an organized system. As it turns out, batch processing is a potent instrument that balances rigidity and adaptability, allowing people to work more intently and productively.

Myths About Multitasking:

The widespread misconception that we can effectively manage several things simultaneously is known as "multitasking." However, scientific data has constantly refuted this idea. Our brains cannot efficiently process multiple complex tasks simultaneously. While basic, automatic behaviors like walking and talking are within our grasp, genuine multitasking, or the ability to do two or more cognitive tasks simultaneously, lowers overall productivity and work quality. The myth about multitasking originates from the false belief that it increases productivity. In actuality, however, it divides our attention, increasing the likelihood of mistakes and stress. Although the brain switches between tasks quickly, a cognitive penalty is associated with this frequent switching. Trying to multitask causes us to lose focus, which makes it difficult to focus on one thing at a time and limits our ability to understand, evaluate, and come up with new ideas. Concentrating on one activity at a time and using batch processing are much better ways to control our workload and get the best results.

Enhancing Attention and In-Depth Work

In the world of productivity, optimizing focus and embracing deep work is like wielding a powerful sword. The key to attaining greatness is the focus or steady attention on a single task. It entails putting all of one's attention into the work, blocking out all outside noise, and letting one's creative and problem-solving abilities run wild. By controlling our attention, we direct our mental energy toward a certain goal, which leads to increased productivity, better quality work, and a deep sense of satisfaction. Cutting through the clutter and pointing us in the direction of mastery and unparalleled productivity is its laser-like precision.

Conversely, deep work is a transformative discipline closely linked to attention. It involves dedicating sizeable, continuous blocks to mentally demanding activities that demand our undivided attention. In this state of intense labor, we make the most use of our brains, exploring complex creativity and problem-solving. Deep work creates a state of flow where time seems to fly by, and the outside world vanishes. By continuously training ourselves to do significant work, we improve our productivity and expand our field knowledge.

Advice Nos. 11 through 15

11- Create and Follow a Budget

This advice is closely related to the others, but a budget is a collection of fundamental guidelines or plans you must follow each month. This budget accounts for your basic living costs and leaves space for savings, debt repayment, and other discretionary spending. Regardless, adhere to the budget.

12- Make Modifications as Required

Life also goes on while you start to budget, save, and pay off debt. Taking a few minutes to review your goals and budget and make any necessary revisions could be beneficial every quarter. This will assist you in sticking to your budget and achieving financial independence. Allow yourself wiggle room for little medical emergencies, problems with your home and car, and other things.

13- Time is Your Priceless Asset.

When it comes to organizing their funds, many people squander their time. Your job's value will become apparent if you recognize that you are exchanging your time for money or compensation. Make an effort to think of ways to maximize the time you spend at work. Look for methods to improve and streamline. You'll succeed in accomplishing this.

14- Use Your Portfolio to Stay Up to Date

You will undoubtedly have a financial advisor if you have reached the stage where you can manage a financial portfolio. Don't believe anything they say. Make it your mission to monitor the performance of your financial portfolio. Try to remain on top of financial matters and learn everything you can to increase the bottom line.

15- Create Extra Before Investing

It could seem alluring to begin investing once you've paid off your debt and accumulated an emergency fund. Doing so is not a smart idea because you wish to have more money saved up before investing. Thanks to the surplus above your emergency money, you have an extra safety net. Additionally, it will help you conserve the money required to make intelligent and profitable investments.

Advice Nos. 16–20

16-Daily List Your Objectives for Financial Freedom

This is a practice that functions similarly to a reaffirmation or daily affirmation. These objectives may vary as life progresses and things occur and alter. This keeps your attention on achieving financial freedom, which you want from life. Simply dedicate five to ten minutes daily to this task and observe your results.

17- Arrange the Budget Two Months at a Time

While monthly budgeting is OK, learning to budget for two months and maintain a one-month cushion is essential if you want to take charge of your money. This will prevent you from overspending this month and ensure you have the money to make all the payments.

18- Request Bill Discounts

If you only inquire, you could be amazed at how many discounts are available. Even utility providers occasionally offer discounts for completing specific tasks. Give them a call and find out if any discounts are available. Credit cards, insurance, and other things are a few that can be useful. Asking for and implementing discounts never hurts.

19- Specify Exactly What You Want

Before taking action, you must have a clear understanding of your aim. You have to be exact when it comes to money matters. Ultimately, money is all about numbers. This contains only entire numbers; there are no halves. Make a detailed list of your intentions and goals, then stick to it with a clear route to success.

20. Don't Cut Your Spending

While it can seem prudent to merely include the bare necessities and leave out expenses like clothing or eating out, this could get you into problems. There will inevitably come moments when you must shell out cash for supper or need new clothing for whatever reason. Make sure you set aside enough money each month for these expenses.

They Don't Make Regular Investments

To begin with, I think it's important for you to understand that saving money won't make you rich. You must put your money to work over an extended period to become wealthy.

Do you know the difference, for example, between wealthy and broke people? While wealthy people earn interest, the poor pay it.

In the end, investing and avoiding debt are the two things you should do if you want to avoid being impoverished. In this manner, interest will be earned for you rather than paid.

Before they save, they spend.

The majority of people are also impoverished because they spend money instead of saving it.

The average person takes their pay, deducts their monthly expenses, and uses the remaining funds for savings and charitable contributions.

The problem is that it increases the pressure to spend rather than save. This ultimately results in a shaky savings account and a delayed path to financial independence.

Reverse the financial process if you want to budget sensibly and steer clear of the common mistakes made by those who are impoverished. Make conserving and giving your money your priority rather than spending it. In short, donate first, save later, and then exit on the remaining funds.

Last Words

The majority of people are broke because they manage their money poorly. I know this because I was one of those people who used to make bad financial judgments. Therefore, it could be time to ask yourself some questions if you find yourself on a ship that looks similar.

● Do you keep an eye on your expenditures and follow a budget?

● Do you prefer making money from investments or paying interest on debt?

● Would you have to take out a loan in case of a medical emergency?

Thankfully, no one is found guilty.

To having no money. It is up to you to shape your financial destiny. Spending money if you have it is OK as long as you have secured a reliable source of income for yourself. You can improve your decision-making and make some effort to turn your finances around.

Acquiring Your Desired Outcome

Even if paying off your debt could take some time, you shouldn't stop living. Understanding the wider picture becomes even more crucial if you start actively managing your funds.

You have done the math. You have kept tabs on your spending. This is the exciting part now.

You need to know the "whys" and the "whats" behind your efforts to manage your finances well and live the life you want.

Why do you wish to improve your financial management? Is it to escape the burden of debt? Is it to avoid worrying about emergencies by having a rainy day fund? Is it to aid with college expenses? These are a few instances of "whys." Is it so that you can purchase additional items? Do you want a superb wedding, a luxurious vacation, a new car, or a house? These would be the "whats" achievable with prudent financial planning.

Understanding your drive and the outcomes you wish to attain is the first step toward success. Your attempts at managing your finances are bound to fail if you don't have a clear objective. Why? They will fall short since managing money necessitates postponing satisfaction.

Consider your feelings after a workday or workweek. You are eager to unwind and enjoy life during your free time, but you have exchanged your time and effort for a salary as payment for your work.

You can go out and enjoy the night with friends if you want to have an amazing vacation in six months, or you can choose to do something cheaper but no less enjoyable, knowing that in six months, you'll be on the trip of a lifetime.

It is far too simple to let "Good Time Charlie" empty your bank account in the name of a nice night out if you don't know why you're taking that large vacation.

There's nothing wrong with Good Time Charlie once in a while, but you have to know when to let him go somewhere else, just like that bothersome friend who offers you their time without considering the possible consequences. Instead of being at his mercy for an unpleasant surprise visit, you are more likely to inform Good Time Charlie when he is welcome and when he is not if you have a goal.

You need to have another talk to counter Good Time, Charlie. You're holding your "Mini Me" here. The small voice inside your head or heart that informs you of everything you aspire to in life is your Mini Me. Mini Me is the one that tells you that you should buy that certain new automobile, go on that dream vacation to Europe, enroll in college, or just stop worrying about how much debt you have.

Mini Me Inventory

It's not better to have vague goals than none at all.

This is an open-minded activity to help you identify exactly what you want to achieve financially. If you want to be as specific as possible about your aims, completing the steps in this exercise will take many days. If you finish everything in an hour, you might not get the most out of this exercise.

We are not talking about a long period of time, even though it can take days. To enable your brain to continue processing what you desire without interruption, it is ideal to complete the tasks in brief, concentrated bursts.

Money is a two-way relationship. It is somewhat an inflow problem and partially an outflow problem. Managing your money involves figuring out how to increase your income and where to spend it to maximize your returns.

This activity is all about you, just like your personal benefits package (like the perks you receive from your employment). This is not for the benefit of others; this is mostly for you. You must do this exercise for yourself before attempting it on someone else if your finances are dependent on them or your family. We'll cover how to take your customized "Mini Me List" and incorporate it into a "Us List" when needed after this part.

FIRST STEP:

Determine the main facets of your existence. These can change according to your tastes and background. These domains generally fit under the following categories: physical, social, emotional/spiritual/mental, and job. Observe that the money category is absent. You will be examining each category through the prism of your aspirations and finances, which is why there isn't a financial category, even though money is one of the most important aspects of life.

Step 2:

Write a single category in large characters at the top of each document. Halve the papers lengthwise. Mark the paper with "What" on the left and "Why" on the right.

Step 3:

Pick a paper and start with the "What." Enumerate whatever you desire. Give it some time. Don't try to prioritize the list or modify yourself. This will be a brainstorming session only. Proceed until the page is filled, or you run out of ideas for over fifteen minutes.

Step Four:

Fill out the "What" column on each category sheet as you see fit. You will eventually address every area of life. Some exercisers find they can finish everything in one sitting by setting out an afternoon or evening. These individuals have previously considered the areas of emphasis and the relationship between them and their financial resources. Taking a break in between steps can be necessary if you haven't given that aspect of your life much thought so that the brain can process what you want.

Step 3: Examine Your Expenses and Keep Your Checkbook Stable

Making sure your expenses don't exceed your income is the goal of budgeting. You should then make changes if they occur and more money is lost than is gained. This doesn't always mean you have to start cutting corners; instead, it's time to take another look at the category of discretionary costs and identify the areas where you can and should cut back.

Your checkbook setup can assist you in keeping track of your investments and outgoing and incoming funds if you make any payments. Although paying with cash is becoming less common, those who continue to use this method should keep their checkbooks balanced. This can save you money on overdraft fees and bounced assessments, and it might also lighten your spending habits.

Step 4: Review your financial situation

After observing your income and outgoings for a few months, you might be more conscious of the areas needing modification. Maybe you underestimated your monthly salary initially, or you neglected to factor in expenses like auto maintenance or veterinary care. Adjust as necessary, but generally speaking, balance inflows and outflows.

Once your budget is finalized, you must commit to sticking to it. Though no financial decision is ever final, fulfillment depends on regular evaluations.

For example, if you purchase merchandise, you can increase both your goals for savings and your discretionary spending. However, a layoff or a reduction in painting hours may require you to cut back on expenditures until your revenues are restored.

A component of the plan should be financial savings. Financial advisors recommend that your savings cover six months' worth of earnings, which should be enough to cover a loss of income or other unforeseen expenses. It can be helpful for you to start a different savings account and gradually fund it until you reach your goal. If you keep a separate account, it will be more difficult to take money out of the emergency fund to pay for non-essential expenses.

Step 5: Commitment

Creating a budget is a wonderful first step toward a more secure financial future for you and your family. You get there by making financial commitments. Remain realistic, assess it often, and don't hesitate to make changes. Stability is the key to budgeting.

Taking care of your finances when unforeseen expenses arise

As mentioned, having an emergency fund is essential for financial security. To begin, help yourself by allocating $50 every week. You will have $2,600 in a year, with interest, in case the transmission blows or the refrigerator breaks down.

Experts advise looking through your withholding taxes to find any unreported income. Suppose you receive a sizable refund each year. In that case, you might want to consider trading in your popularity as a submitter to receive additional funds from your paycheck, which you might put toward an emergency fund. Unless this is the case, you're putting your tax return budget into that fund.

Particularly in the case of scientific problems, a balanced budget can go south. Haggle with the health center about expensive medical bills, such as those for an emergency sanatorium stay. Charges are negotiated in almost all hospitals. Usually, the hospital or business can set up a payment plan if you contact them right away rather than waiting until the money is due to be collected.

If not, you can combine all of your scientific payments into a single monthly invoice through an organization or a mortgage from a financial institution using a scientific invoice consolidation, which can help. Although you can pay your payments on time, the organization still safeguards your credit score rating even though this no longer makes things easier for you. The drawback is that it can take longer for you to finish paying off your debt.

The advantages of creating a budget

Everyone can gain from managing their finances in a proactive and recommended manner. Committing your finances will help you advance into a more lucrative career.

You can have a better life by budgeting because:

Well-known displays of trash. Expanding finances highlights things that many people overlook daily.

Sets priorities. With the help of a budget, people can have a clear picture of their spending patterns and establish new objectives to make the most of their financial resources.

Produces novel behavior. People can move prices into certain classifications and become more aware of unnecessary spending when they understand how they have used their money.

Lessens tension. One of the most stressful environments is the financial one. Even though there is a sense of control over the money coming in and going out, the tension can eventually become a feeling of empowerment.

Teaches. A finance degree enables people to see money as a tool and shift their perspective to long-term goals and desires for the future.

The first step in managing your finances is creating them, but the real growth and increased value for your money come from maintaining them. Maintaining a strong financial mindset is essential since adhering to a budget can be challenging for individuals who aren't accustomed to spending limits or strong financial resolve.

Maintaining your influence might help relieve some of the stress associated with budgeting. To ensure you have enough money for a relaxing trip at the end of the year, consider setting aside a small amount each month.

Set reasonable objectives eventually. Start cautiously and work your way up to a strategy that suits your needs and way of life.

The more refined elements

Desires versus Wants

One of the Rolling Stones' well-known anthems from the 1960s, "You May Continue to Get What You Want," speaks to a problem that many of us deal with daily. The lesson is that even though you might not be able to acquire the things you desire if you work hard enough, you can still obtain what you need.

Why bother, and how do you distinguish needs from wishes? For many of us, understanding where to draw the line might mean the difference between building a profitable business and going bankrupt. What makes the difference, then? Maximum wishes are equivalent to non-voluntary expenses. They include housing, which necessitates paying for a mortgage or rent, and food, which results in grocery bills. Numerous additional things might be basic and non-negotiable, yet the non-negotiable group is flexible.

For example, you can buy a new BMW or a used Kia sedan if you require a car to travel to the paintings. The Beemer is guaranteed to electrify your friends and offer an amazing utilization experience, and the price difference is substantial. What you can afford is the question. You can probably buy the BMW without straining your finances if you earn $500k a year. However, continuing driving the Kia is preferable if your income is $40,000.

The same goes for a house: is it better to buy a $400,000 house or rent a one-bedroom condo? Once more, both provide a safe refuge, albeit at astronomically high prices.

Additionally, there is a distinction between desires and devices that you could live without. Consider traveling to Thailand for a vacation rather than visiting state parks nearby for a week. While each can offer enjoyable and tranquil spots to spend time downtown, the costs are distinctly different. Additionally, consider impulsive purchases. Imagine you visit a home improvement store to pick up some lawn fertilizer and come out with a lawnmower you hadn't planned to purchase. Even if you might require a new mover, it's a great idea to look at prices and styles before making a commitment.

What Are Some Fundamentals We Should Understand Before Investing In Options Trading?

How to Begin Trading Options Day Trading

You should be well-informed about a few things before making your decisions about day-exchanging business. These are your current financial situation, the amount of time you can devote to day trading, and your level of risk tolerance. Create a financial accounting report that lists your expenses and any additional compensation you receive. Health and the degree to which you can allocate resources to decisions. This also helps you to understand the risks involved in making trade-offs. Never exchange above your level of experience in exchanging, and never contribute money or assets that you cannot afford to lose. Being an informed investor in your own right needs some serious time investment up front as you want to become an expert in this area and build a strong foundation for your portfolio. Avoid rushing into things and throwing away money in an eager attempt to get going.

Next, learn how to exchange options on paper before risking your hard-earned money. This is known as paper swapping, and it allows you to assess your presentation in terms of exchanging possibilities by using real-world scenarios.

When you're ready to advance to continuous practice, watch a business company to assist you. But make sure you thoroughly investigate the company to ensure its reputation and that you are paying the lowest possible commissions. It may even be possible for you to watch an agent in action who doesn't take commissions.

The finance company will help you set up the appropriate documentation and help you become a certified choices dealer at the level appropriate for your experience. Before you go to a broker, you ought to be able to handle payments and other financial transactions online. Finally, make sure you have the tools needed for the trade. Make sure your web connection is reliable and fast. Additionally, since trading applications depend on a rapid PC, make sure yours has a fast processor and enough memory to prevent problems. Most dealers require at least two displays to stay informed about developments in the financial market.

The simple solution is to start with very little exchange and a great deal of tolerance. A dealer needs to arrange execution properly. The broker should educate themselves on the market, take a position, maintain it, and work to become competent, focused, and successful traders.

Unpredictability

If everything goes wrong and you cannot sell your contracts on time, this is the total amount you could lose.

Throughout the term of the agreement, the choices contract's premium would fluctuate. It would keep evolving. Factors such as the current exchange rate's adjustment to the strike value, the volatility of the market, and the amount of time left until expiration will all play a role.

As a result, the buyer's primary goal should remain to obtain the choice agreement at the lowest possible price. This will provide you the best chance to get out of the trade with the least loss or gain. It would be harder for you to exit the transaction with a smaller profit if you purchased it at a higher price.

The stock is said to be volatile if it generally exhibits sudden developments. This increases the choices dealer's risk. The dealer raises the premium by factoring a stock's unpredictable nature to the risk assessment.

But there's a problem with the computation of instability. Most of the time, the verifiable presentation of the stock determines the instability. This suggests that the selected merchant may speculate about the stock's long-term volatility, which could lead to an inaccurate estimate of unpredictability. However, this will still result in a rise in premium pricing.

This unstable figure may alter as the stock's trading peaks and the agreed-upon amount of time passes, affecting the premium's value in the process.

Let's use a model to better understand this:

Let us assume that a stock is trading at $100. The expiration date is in 30 days.

In the call option, the strike price is $130.

The superior worth will rise if the implied instability is half, as the selections dealer will consider this factor and factor it into the premium.

But now, the stock probably won't be that erratic.

As a result, the buyer of the options contract ought to examine the diagrams' current level of stock volatility. Assuming there is no extraordinary volatility in the stock, it is unlikely that addressing a substantial expense on the premium will be genuinely prudent. It is important to remember that the inferred unpredictability (IV) rate also increases the choice contract's external worth or time esteem.

Utilize

When you begin using leverage, it may be a thrilling tool. The capacity to generate far more profit than you could through influence is highly useful and fascinating. However, before you employ leverage, there are two things you should be aware of. Make sure you have enough assets to cover every penny of edge you use without touching the money supporting your life or trading career, first and foremost. If you lose all the money in that deal, $5,000 will need to be available to cover the influence, assuming you acknowledge a 10:1 influence on $500. Specifically, you want to have that $5,000 without truly compromising the ability to support your life or future exchanges.

Additionally, be aware of your specialist's edge-call technique. When are they distributed? Where are the edges? How often were they previously administered? Since you have no control over the market, you have no say in whether your specialist calls your edge. Right now, all that's left to do is learn about them and take the appropriate precautions.